# CRYSTAL **HEALING** & THE **HUMAN** **ENERGY** FIELD

## A Beginner's Guide

## Marion McGeough
### British Academy of Reiki

First published in Great Britain in 2013

Published by Marion McGeough

A catalogue record for this book is available from the British Library.

# CONTENTS

# ABOUT THE AUTHOR

Marion McGeough is a Reiki Master, Psychotherapist and Hypnotherapist. Founder of the British Academy of Reiki, she teaches Reiki in Sutton Coldfield, West Midlands and Ashby de la Zouch, Leicestershire and is currently working on a series of hypnotherapy CDs due for release in the coming months. She lives in the Midlands with her husband, 3 dogs and two cats.

# A WORLD OF VIBRATION AND ENERGY

**H**ave you ever walked into a room and felt that there was a great atmosphere present with people in the room smiling, laughing and generally having a good time? I bet you have. The opposite is also true. Most of us have been to places which seemed to drain our energy and we just can't wait to leave. The Law of Vibration shows that everything is made up of energy. Science and metaphysics agree that everything: people, animals, plants and objects such as crystals are composed of particles of energy which vibrate at specific frequencies or speeds.

As everything is made up from energy there is really no difference between you, the chair you may be sitting on at this moment and me, as I sit typing the draft of this book on my computer. The reason that we feel that we are separate from all around us is due to the different frequencies that people, animals and objects are vibrating at. It is, therefore, a natural conclusion that there is no difference between you or me. We are one as we share the same energy. This energy is not static but dynamic and is constantly changing. As particles of energy vibrate it is our thoughts, feelings and actions which can alter these vibrations. When we are feeling low we emit a low vibrational frequency and when we are feeling happy and full of life we emit a much higher frequency.

We have all met people who seem to find life easy. The things that they want seem to come to them without effort. These people are often successful in whatever they do; they have an abundance of money and friends and they seem to attract more of the same as they go through life. These people are vibrating at a high frequency and like a magnet they are attracting more of the same. Like attracts like: this is the Law of Attraction.

Have you ever jumped out of bed at the sound of your alarm clock and in your haste to get to the bathroom you stubbed your toe and said to yourself: "This is going to be a bad day"? Well, what did you find? Yes, the day WAS a bad day for you. You may have missed the bus or train to work, or been held up in a traffic jam. Your boss kept piling up the work and your colleagues all seemed in a bad mood. At lunch time you have a few minutes to yourself, you think back to the early morning when you were getting out of bed and you focus on the first thought that you had this morning, which was that it was going to be a bad day and you were right. Does this mean that you have some hidden ability or sixth sense? No. What this really means is that you began the day on a low vibrational frequency and carried on that way. Throughout the day you attracted people and situations to you that also had a low vibrational frequency and therefore you attracted more of the same. All of the people you came into contact with also came into contact with this low vibrational frequency and their energy or vibrations began to operate at a lower frequency. So the energy in the office, the factory or wherever you work becomes lower and lower, until all around you are feeling miserable and in a bad mood. Does this mean that your day is doomed to failure and that it may have been better for you to snuggle up under the duvet and go back to sleep? No. You have the ability to change your vibrational frequency, just as you have the ability to change the television channel if you start watching a programme you do not like. The Law of attraction states that by changing the way you think you will change the frequency of the vibrations. This, in turn, will change what you attract to you in your life.

As well as paying attention to our thoughts and being aware of the energy and vibrations around us, we need to pay attention to our physical environment. If we are unhappy with how and where we live it is wise to pay attention to our thoughts and take notice of what is it we are lacking. With our physical environment some people have a preference to be by water, others the sea or mountains. Now it may not be physically possible to move to our desired location or environment due to family commitments, job, finances and numerous other reasons, but we can take time out to visit our chosen environment as often as possible. It is not a co-incidence that the person who has arthritis and back pain goes on holiday and comments that the pain and stiffness in the joints just seems to have disappeared. Our vibrations are at their highest when we are in the best environment for us and when we are happy and stress free.

For many the work environment causes much stress and ill health. Offices, factories and even hospitals are often grey and bland, lacking natural sunlight and fresh air. The stress of having targets to reach and a peak performance to maintain are now sadly part of everyday life, along with the boredom and repetition of tasks which "need" to be carried out on a day to day basis. Few people are passionate about what they do and lack the energy and vitality that is required for optimal health and a great life. When a person is living a life or working in a job they are unhappy with, this energy becomes blocked and dis-ease begins to manifest. I am sure we can all remember an activity or lesson at school that we did not enjoy. For me it was physical education and I would often develop a tummy ache before this lesson began. Another lesson I hated was maths and I would feel physically sick just before this lesson. Now I am sure that most of you can relate to how I was feeling just before maths and physical education. Now imagine what it is like to be living a life, working in a job or being in a situation that you do not like month after month, year after year. Think of the effects this stress has on the physical body and why it is not just desirable but essential to make the changes necessary to bring yourself back into balance.

Now that there is an increasing interest in complimentary therapies such a reflexology, reiki, energy work and crystals there has never been a better time to help support your body by increasing its energy and life force. This guide will show you a number of ways that you can use crystals to increase your vibrations and energy, as well as how to select and take care of the beautiful crystals you have chosen to bring into your life.

# HOW TO SELECT YOUR CRYSTALS

There are a number of ways you can select your crystals for healing:

- You can choose the crystals which correspond to the condition(s) you wish to treat by looking them up in a book.

- You can choose the crystals by their appearance by choosing the ones which are the most attractive.

- You may be given a crystal by a friend as a gift.

- You can choose your crystals intuitively.

Choosing a crystal by using your intuition is the best way of acquiring it. Each crystal has its own colour, vibration and function. When you feel drawn to a crystal, in order to establish if it is really for you, place it in the palm of your hand and close your eyes. The vibration from the crystal and your vibrations will connect raising you to a higher frequency. You may see pictures or colours if you connect deeply with it. If the crystal is not for you at this particular time you may have a strong feeling that something is not quite right or you simply may not connect with its vibrations. It is important to remember that the crystal will only stay with you for as long as you need its energy. Often people report that they have lost their crystal and simply do not know where it has gone. A Crystal will return to the earth or the sea when its work has been done.

# WHERE TO PURCHASE YOUR CRYSTALS

## Three popular methods of purchasing crystals

Many people purchase their crystals online as this can be cheaper than buying them from a shop or they may be able to purchase a rare type of crystal which is not available to them locally. I do not recommend this method of purchasing crystals for the beginner crystal healer for two reasons. Firstly, you are unable to really connect with the crystal to discover if it is able and willing to work with you. Secondly, you are not able to assess the quality of the stone in order to establish if there are any cracks or flaws present. However, that said, there are many companies which have an excellent reputation for providing quality crystals and whose businesses operate online. There are also individuals who are very intuitive and can choose a crystal which will work very well for them simply by looking at the online photograph. With time and experience the beginner will become more intuitive and sensitive in selecting the right crystals for their work.

Another popular way in which people purchase crystals is to buy them at events and shows. This may be an excellent way of purchasing interesting and unusual crystals. When buying crystals in this way, please be aware that many people may have handled the crystals and their individual energy and vibrations can affect the frequency at which the crystal is vibrating. When selecting crystals at events, always take a little longer when connecting with the crystal to ensure that it is right for you.

Purchasing crystals at specialised shops or retail units is the best way of selecting your crystals. When purchasing in this way there is often an abundance of stones to choose from and specialised knowledge may be available. You are able to select and inspect the stones. Some shops may even be able to source a particular stone for you and you can inspect the quality and discover if you can connect with it before buying.

# HOW TO CLEANSE YOUR CRYSTALS

**W**hen a crystal comes into your possession it is always very important to cleanse it first before using or displaying it. By cleansing the crystal you are removing any build- up of negative energy and giving the crystal a "fresh start". Crystals that are not cleansed lose their sparkle over time and become tired and look faded. A crystal which has been bought from a shop may have sat on the shelf for a while collecting dust. Dust is drawn to the crystals via the crystals electromagnetic properties. The dust will affect the crystals ability to heal as well as making it less attractive to the eye.

Overleaf are some ways in which crystals can be cleansed:

*Water*

**Free Running Water:** You can place the crystals in a sink with the tap running for thirty minutes. This is a good option if the crystals are cleansed on a regular basis and just look a bit cloudy. If you are fortunate to live near a stream you may choose to place the crystals in a "safe place" so that they are not dragged down stream but receive a lovely cascade of pure, fresh water to cleanse them.

**Bowl of water:** Place the crystals in a bowl of water and leave them there for between two to four hours if cleansed on a regular basis and up to twenty four hours if newly purchased.

**Salt:** Sea salt is ideal but if this not available you can use ordinary cooking salt. It is important to remember that you must throw away any salt that you use to cleanse crystals and not use it for cooking or anything else. This is because the salt absorbs negative energies from the crystals and you certainly do not want to ingest this negative energy.

**Dry Salt:** Place the crystals in a bowel of dry salt and leave them overnight.

**Salt & water:** Place half a mug full of salt in a bowl of water. Stir so that the salt makes contact with the water. Place the crystals in the bowl and leave overnight.

***Important:*** *It is not suitable for some crystals to be cleansed in salt and the salt can change the properties and even the shape of some crystals. Opal, Lapis Lazuli and Pyrite should NEVER be cleansed in salt. If in doubt, leave salt out.*

**Burying Crystals:** You can bury the crystal in the earth. Just remember where you have buried it! Leave the crystal there for between one day and one week. The crystal will be cleansed deeply. However, beware – if the crystal is not for you it may simply vanish and no matter how hard you look you will not be able to find it. The crystal has gone back to the earth from where it came.

**Moonlight:** Leave the crystal out during a full moon. The next day the crystal will be fully cleansed and rejuvenated.

**Smudging:** Burn a smudge stick of sage and pass the smoke through the crystal. As the smoke passes through the crystal ask for the crystal to be cleansed. This process will remove any negative energy.

**Brushing:** Use a fine brush and gently dust the crystal as part of your domestic cleaning routine.

# NOW BEGIN WORKING WITH CRYSTALS

**N**ow that you have selected and cleansed your crystals it is time to begin to work with them. The first step is to begin to connect with each individual crystal. You can do this by:

Finding a quiet place where you will not be disturbed. This may be a room or space within your house or, if the weather is fine, perhaps in the garden. Ensure that you will not be disturbed by requesting that other household members do not disturb you and remember to turn off the telephones and mobile phones. If you are able to go into the garden make sure that it is not a time when your neighbour will pop their head over the fence for a chat or when someone is mowing the lawn!

If you are able, sit on the floor/ ground with your legs crossed. If you do not wish to do this or if you have a physical restriction then it is perfectly fine to sit on a chair with your feet flat on the floor.

Turn on some calming and relaxing music if you enjoy listening to music.

Close your eyes and take a few deep breaths.

When you are ready, place the crystal in the palm of the right hand and say to yourself: "I respectfully ask you to help me heal."

Keep the crystal in the palm of your right hand for three to four minutes.

Now repeat this exercise holding the crystal in the palm of your left hand.

Open your eyes and take a deep breath in and out and just relax.

Now reflect on the sensations you felt. Were they different in each hand or very much the same? Could you feel the vibrations of the crystal and if so were those vibrations quick and pulsating or a little heavy and dense? There may be times when a crystal feels too strong and powerful for you to use at this particular moment in time. If this is the case then you may wish to place the crystal near direct sunlight in your home and allow its energy to vibrate within your home until both you and the crystal are able to work together. From time to time you can pick the crystal up and hold it to see if you are able to notice any changes in vibrational energy and, of course, from time to time please ensure that you cleanse and dust the crystal so that it does not become tired and ineffective.

# PROGRAMMING CRYSTALS USING REIKI

**F**or those people who are lucky enough to work with reiki there are a number of ways in which reiki can be used to help programme crystals after the crystal has been cleansed using one of the above methods.

To begin, for those who are reiki masters or who are familiar with the Tibetan Master symbol. The symbol can be drawn over the crystal followed by the name of the symbol being repeated three times to empower it. The reiki worker then imagines the symbol being passed right through the crystal thoroughly cleaning any negative energy from it.

For those who like working with symbols, after the crystal has been cleansed and depending on the work it has been asked to carry out, the crystal can be programmed with Cho-Ku-Rei to aid with physical healing or to help ground a person. Alternately, the crystal can be programmed with

Sei-He-ki if the work it is required to carry out is one which is more emotional or mental in nature.

For those reiki workers who are intuitive: The crystal can be programmed by drawing down reiki from the crown of the head and feeling the energy cascade all the way down to the arms and into the hands where the crystal is being held. Ask the crystal to help heal the particular person it is being programmed for. Focus on this person and ask the crystal to help heal them to the best of its ability. Once you have finished healing work with the specific individual involved, thoroughly cleanse the crystal and say a silent thank you to it for assisting you in carrying out the healing.

## Using the Reiki Kotodama

For those students of reiki who are at second degree or beyond and have moved on from using symbols, or have become familiar with the Reiki kotodama, you will find that you are able to chant these sacred sounds to evoke changes in the energy and change the vibrations of the crystals. As you continue to chant, either silently to yourself or by chanting out loud, changes in vibrations will occur within any crystals you are holding. The kotodama were used in ancient Japan by those who believed that words and sounds had mystical powers and could evoke changes, not only within a person, but changes in the environment. It has even been said that wars and whole armies could be stopped after the relevant chanting had begun. The sound of each vowel is considered to evoke a specific energy or vibration so, when a word is said, a connection is made with the source which will emit a specific type of energy leading to changes in the person, any object they are holding or the environment.

## Practical Exercise

Take a thoroughly cleansed crystal and place it in your dominant reiki hand. If you are uncertain as to which hand this is, it is the hand which emits the most heat and which is sensitive to any changes in energy that you feel or experience when working on clients, family and friends.

Take a few deep breathes and now begin by imagining reiki flowing or cascading down from the crown chakra all the way down your head and arms into your hands.

Say silently to yourself: "I wish to empower this crystal with Cho Ku Rei energy".

Cho Ku Rei is the Reiki Symbol for the focus Kotodama. The sound for the focus Kotodama is: Ho Ku Ei.

Now begin by chanting the Focus Kotodama. Begin by taking a deep breath in and as you exhale chant the Kotodama. Continue chanting for between three and five minutes. As time passes you may notice:

## Changes in your own energy system.

You become at one with the Cho Ku Rei energy. You may feel heavier and rooted to the floor as you become more grounded. If you felt tired before you begin chanting you may feel refreshed afterwards and more alert.

## Changes in the Tanden.

This is your energy centre, the centre of your whole being and where your focus is when you meditate. You may feel a tingling, or buzzing sensation in the Tanden or you may feel nothing at all. Each experience is individual; however, if you do not feel anything at all this does not mean that it is not working, it simply means that you need to focus more on meditations to increase the sensations in your Tanden.

## Changes in the Energy of the crystal

You may feel that the energy that the crystal emits has changed. The crystal may have become heavier and feel more solid in the palm of your hand.

Now end the Kotodama meditation by taking a deep breath in and as you exhale say silently to yourself: "I now end this meditation and am thankful for the energy received".

The crystal can be used whenever you need it to emit Cho Ku Rei energy. Remember that once the crystal has been cleansed it will need to be re-programmed before use again.

# HEALING USING THE CHAKRA SYSTEM

The word "Chakra" derives from the Sanskrit word "Cakra", meaning wheel or disc. Chakras are spinning wheels of light or energy. The Sanskrit language is one of the Indic languages of India and the language itself dates back to around 1500 BC or possibly earlier. The word Sanskrit when translated can mean complete, perfect or pulled together depending on the translation. The Chakras were first mentioned in ancient Hindu texts when it was suggested that it is possible to awaken these energies through meditation.

There are seven major Chakra points in the body and numerous minor ones. The Chakras are part of the subtle body; this is an energy system which is not visible to the naked eye for most people. The Chakras cannot be detected by an x-Ray machine and they do not play a part in modern medicine.

For those of us who are fortunate enough to have developed the sixth sense it may be possible to see each individual Chakra spinning, as well as the speed it is spinning at and the colour of it. Chakras are wheels of energy. Each has an opening which projects several inches from the physical body; this opening spins and takes in universal life energy. This in turn distributes the energy to the body and specific organs that it is related to. If the energy becomes blocked the chakra will slow down and eventually stop spinning if left untreated. The life force of the person becomes depleted, leading to illness. Each chakra has a small tip which holds it in place at the spine. It is also possible to use your intuition and sense to get a feel of a particular Chakra and to determine the health of it.

# CHAKRA EXERCISE

**F**ind a quiet place to sit where you will not be disturbed for several minutes. Play some relaxing music if this will help you switch off from any outside noises.

When you are ready, focus your attention on the area between the middle of the neck and the collar bone. This is the Throat Chakra.

Using your senses you can either:

Visualise the area.

Note any feelings or sensations.

Experience any sounds or noises which the Chakra sends you. (Some people hear sounds of the wind blowing gently or the sounds of a storm).

When you are ready you can open your eyes.

This exercise does take practice so please do not become disappointed with yourself if you have not experienced very much the first time you carry it out. If you carry out any form of meditation on a regular basis, this exercise will be easier for you than for someone who is new to the practice. If you found that the chakra was spinning too fast and appeared wide open you may be an excitable and over talkative person who can display an arrogant trait at times. If the Chakra was spinning too slowly you may be a person who holds back and is unable to speak their mind and express their feelings. If the Chakra is in balance you will find that it was spinning at an even and steady pace. This indicates that you are a good communicator. The colour of the Chakra should be a bright blue. If the Chakra is spinning too slowly it may be a murky blue in colour.

Now that you have some insight into the health of your throat chakra you may wish to carry out the chakra exercise with the other 6 major chakras, the names and locations are listed below:

### The crown chakra
This is located at the top of your head and is associated with spirituality.

### The Brow Chakra
This is located in the middle of the forehead, between the eyebrows. This area is known as the Third Eye.

### The Heart Chakra
This is located in the middle of the chest. This is the centre of what makes us human: love, empathy and compassion.

## The Solar Plexus Chakra

This is located just below the breastbone. This is our emotional centre.

## The Sacral Chakra

This is located just below the navel. This is the centre of creativity. In some cultures and traditions this is also the centre of a person's life force.

## The Base Chakra

This is located at the base of the spine. This is home to our connection to the earth and this is why we feel an affinity for nature.

Now that you have an increased awareness of, or feeling for, your chakras, you may have detected an imbalance in one or more chakras. You may have felt that the chakra was spinning either to fast or too slow. For each chakra I have selected 4 different crystals which can be used to balance the chakras.

## The Crown Chakra

Health problems: when out of balance: lack of self-awareness which at times leads to depression, fatigue ME, fibromyalgia, frustration, conditions of the skin such as eczema. Eventually the nervous stem is affected as the body becomes over leaded.

## Crystals:

Amethyst (helps along the spiritual path)

Howlite (this is the birthstone of Gemini – this helps insomnia and fatigue)

Spirit Quartz (helps in decision making – helps you make the right choices in life).

Clear Quartz (assists the work of the other crystals increases healing and balances the chakras).

## The Brow Chakra

Health Problems: Fatigue, mental illness and confusion, indecision, learning difficulties and problems assimilating information, lack of drive and lack of interest in life.

## Crystals:

Lapis Lazuli (helps to release painful and harmful memories)

Sodalite (helps thoughts flow easily and clearly)

Tanzanite (helps increase feelings of connection, love and compassion and all things that make us human and helps support emotional healing)

Herkimer Diamond (a very high vibration stone which aids the other crystals and helps astral projection).

## The Throat Chakra

Health Problems : Digestive problems, bowel

problems - either too sluggish or too frequent, skin rashes and complaints, mental health problems affecting communication – the inability to verbally express oneself to others due to fear of inadequacy, heart problems due to a build-up of suppressed emotions.

## Crystals:
Blue Lace Agate (Aids communication, connects with higher self.)

Aquamarine (Assists the release of suppressed emotions, heals release fear, and aids balance.)

Blue Quartz (Helps protect the user from negativity, helps heal the physical body and supports the immune system.)

Blue Apatite Stone (Increases spirituality and aids a relaxed mind, increase self- awareness and spirituality.)


## The Heart Chakra
Health Problems: Emotional confusion, a "cold" personality, heart disease, repeated coughs, colds and chest infections, respiratory problems such as asthma, COPD.

## Crystals:

Emerald (Once worn by pregnant women as it was said to protect the unborn baby; emerald is used for healing infections, eliminating fevers and preventing disease. Emeralds also help release negative emotions.)

 Green Jade (This assists the release of emotions and assists feelings of love and nurturing. Jade helps assist the kidneys and adrenal glands to eliminate toxins and the removal of waste products, thus cleansing the body.)

Rose Quartz (This helps to aids in the release of emotions by opening up the heart to the "good" feelings of love, trust, friendship and compassion. This crystal also helps remove negativity, grief and any blocked or "stuck" emotions.)

Ruby (Helps by assisting emotional healing of the heart; promotes drive and positive emotions and protects the user from negative energy.)


## The Solar Plexus Chakra

Health Problems: Poor sleeping problems, stress, eating disorders and anxiety. If the chakra is spinning too fast an individual may be arrogant, consumed and driven by success. If the chakra is spinning too slowly an individual may be fearful, indecisive and lacking confidence.

## Crystals:

Citrine (This helps reduce stress and remove negative energy. It helps to promote feelings of creativity and honesty and other positive emotions and feelings.)

Amber (This stone is a powerful healing and cleansing stone, helping to clear the nervous system and promote wellbeing. Amber also absorbs pain and negative energy.)

Beryl (This stone aids balance. It also aids circulation, absorbs pain and has a subtle effect on the mind by helping balance the individual by removing stress. Beryl also helps eliminate gastro-intestinal problems and enhances the immune system.)

Tigers Eye (This stone helps remove mental blocks by removing stress and tension and aiding clarity and vision. This stone helps to protect and prevent energy depletion.)

## The Sacral Chakra

Health Problems: If this chakra is out of balance a person may experience any of a number of issues ranging from kidney problems, sexual health problems, and attachment disorders. A person may be too cold and distant or too clingy and needy. Back pain and eating disorders are also commonly found in those whose sacral chakra is out of balance.

## Crystals:

Copper (This stone is great for aiding balance; it helps to ground a person and creates clarity and vision.)

Pearl (This assists the digestive system, helps to reduce or eliminate stomach problems and helps to strengthen the immune system.)

Orange Calcite (This stone helps to release unhealthy emotions and increases energy. It helps by offering protection and improving intuition.)

Moonstone (This stone helps to stimulate the function of the pineal gland and balances the hormonal cycle. Moonstone helps to promote good fortune in both an individual's personal life and in business. It offers protection both on land and sea.)

## The Base or Root Chakra

Health Problems: This chakra is found in the base of the spine and is known to emit the lowest vibration as it works on the slowest wavelength. If this chakra is not spinning correctly a person may experience back pain including sciatica, varicose veins, water retention, constipation, diarrhoea as well as problems with the immune system and phobias.

## Crystals:

Red Jasper (This is one of the oldest stones. It

offers protection against hazards of the night and promotes stability. It encourages a person to speak out.)

Smokey Quartz (This stone is grounding and helps to neutralise negative vibrations. This stone offers protection and helps a person to detoxify as well as supporting the digestive system, eliminating nightmares and supports a person's ability to concentrate and freely express their emotions.)

Black Amber (This stone is formed from fossilised wood. Black amber offers powerful protection and helps to ward off evil and psychic attacks. For those suffering with depression, this stone helps to lift those feelings by clearing the mind and helping a person to see solutions to their problems.)

Petrified Wood (This is, just like black amber: fossilised wood. This stone offers a great deal of grounding and protection and helps a person to distinguish what is important in one's life. This stone assists with slow and gradual change.)

# A STEP-BY-STEP GUIDE TO CHAKRA HEALING

Prepare: Use a quiet healing space where you will not be disturbed. Make sure that your crystals are cleansed, if necessary, and ready for use. Try to use a height adjustable couch if possible rather than a bed or similar. You need to make sure that you are comfortable and that you are not bending too low or are positioning yourself in difficult to negotiate positions. Protect your back from potential injuries at all times. You may wish to cleanse the room by burning some sage. You may also decide to use candles and play relaxing music.

The client:  Ask your client to remove any chunky jewellery including watches and belts. Ask the client to remove their shoes and to lie on the couch. You may need to adjust the height of the head position of the couch especially if the client has breathing problems. Ask if it is acceptable to cover the client's legs, below the waist, with a thin blanket. Not only will this keep the client warm it will aid relaxation, but it will not affect the quality of the healing.

Your Crystals: To begin with choose one crystal mentioned elsewhere in this guide for each of the chakras. You may also chose to supplement these by purchasing a number of small clear quartz crystals. These crystals will strengthen and support the work of the other crystals making the healing process more powerful as well as drawing out negative energy.

## Place Your Crystals

Begin by placing your main or chosen crystals over each of the chakras. Carry this out in the following sequence:

*Crown:*              This is at the top of the head.

*Brow:*               Middle of the forehead.

*Throat:*             Middle of the throat.

*Heart:*              Middle of the chest.

*Solar Plexus:*       At the base of the breastbone.

*Sacral:*             Just below the naval.

*Base (or root):* At the bottom of the spine – place the crystal in between the legs below the client's private parts.

*Optional: If you have decided to use the clear quartz crystals to support your healing you can place them now. Begin at the crown chakra and work your way down just as in the above sequence. Please small clusters of clear quartz around the main healing crystal for each of the chakras.*

## Healing Duration

If this is your client's first experience with chakra healing, 15 to 30 minutes is advised. Check on your client after 10 minutes. Often the client will be asleep. Occasionally a crystal will be too strong for the client causing discomfort. If this does happen simply remove the crystal but do not replace with another as this will disturb the treatment. You can gradually work up to 55 minutes over a course of treatments. At times you may find that a crystal has fallen off the client onto the couch; please leave the crystal on the couch. It is often the case that the crystal has done as much work as it can with the client for the time being or it may be that the particular crystal is not suitable for the client. Note which crystal it is and if it happens again select another crystal.

**End Of session:** Begin by gently waking the client if they are asleep by touching their arm and stating that the treatment has ended. Now remove the main crystals and then the clear quartz if you have used them.

Help the client off the couch if necessary and offer them a drink of water. Give the client time to gather their thoughts; crystal chakra healing can be very powerful and the client may feel as if he or she has just woken up from a deep sleep. Make notes of any relevant comments such as dreams, sensations or other feelings the client may have experienced. This may help you choose what crystals to use in any future treatments as well as deepening your understanding of the healing properties of crystals as you practice and gain experience. Give the client a small clear quartz crystal to carry with them, this will help to support healing and keep any negative thoughts at a distance.

**Cleansing:** When the client has left, cleanse the crystals with your chosen method. Cleanse the room by burning a sage bundle or, if you are familiar with the reiki symbols, use the Tibetan Master symbol to cleanse the room.

With experience you will begin to develop the use of your intuition and you will instinctively choose the right crystals for your client. You must be patient as this requires practice and self-awareness.

# THE AURA

## What is the Aura?

The human energy field is made up of seven layers which project outwards from the human body at various distances. Each level is connected to the body by the skin. Each level is made up of a higher vibrational frequency than that of the previous layer. Individuals who have psychic ability are able to see some or all of the layers of the aura. Some may be able to see a fine greyish, white or bluish mist others who may be especially gifted, may see all of the layers in detail.

Animals, plants and even objects have an aura as everything in and of our world are made of vibrations. I am sure many of you may have seen specialist photographs during your science class which show a plant with a leaf removed from it. The photograph from the aura of the plant shows it whole and complete with a fine white or yellow line showing where the cut off or removed part would have been. Amputees often experience pain or sensation where a removed limb once was. This is not because they are pining for what they once had, rather, it is because in their subconscious mind the limb is still present, as it is in the auric field.

## The 7 Layers of the Aura

The seven layers of the aura relate to the emotional, spiritual and physical state or condition of the person. As a person is constantly feeling, interacting with and experiencing their environment, subtle changes within the auric field take place all of the time. When any damage is done within the subtle energy field by stress or negative thoughts and feelings the aura will become damaged and holes will appear. These holes will let in more negative energy until the physical body becomes affected resulting in dis-ease. It is the aim of healers and crystal healers to repair the holes in the energy field and to release any blockages, thereby restoring good health and natural balance to the individual. The energy field can be felt by moving your hands parallel to the body, in this way you will feel the etheric body. You may feel areas of built up energy which will need to be released and in some areas you may feel that the energy is fine or light. This may be an area where there is a hole in the aura. Given time, you may be able to feel the other areas of the aura as your psychic and intuitive ability increases. Healers and light energy workers, whose hands have become sensitive to the energy, should find this exercise easy.

**The Etheric Body** - This is the layer which is closest to the body. It is situated between 1 and 5 cm from the body. The etheric body is connected to the physical body. Damage to the etheric body will result in physical illness or dis-ease.

**The Emotional Body** – This is 5 to 10 cm away from the skin. This is connected with our feelings, thoughts and emotions. This layer is closely connected to the physical body. If we experience negative or distressing thoughts and emotions on a regular basis the emotional body becomes damaged and this, in time affects the etheric body before we display physical symptoms of illness.

**The Mental Body** – This is situated between 10 and 20 cm from the skin. This layer represents our thoughts, emotions and values. This represents our rational mind. This layer represents our intellect and is part of our higher level thoughts.

**The Astral Body** - This is situated between 20 and 30 cm from the skin. This layer contains that part of ourselves which represents unconditional love for people, the environment, plants and animals. This layer is the bridge between the physical plane and the mental plane. Any damage in this area will result in feelings of lack of connection, self-hate and loathing.

**The Etheric Temple** - This is situated between 30 and 40 cm from the skin. This layer is connected to our ability to communicate. It is within this level that our higher-self connects with the spiritual plane.

**The Intuitive Body** - This is situated between 60 and 90 cm away from the skin. This layer contains all of our intuitive thoughts, feelings and emotions. If we feel uncomfortable in the close presence of another person, even if they are not physically touching us, it is our intuitive body that is telling us that something is not quite right.

**The Causal Body** - This is situated between 90 and 190 cm from the skin and contains our spiritual aspect, divine knowledge. This is our higher-self and what we hope to become or achieve.

# HEALING
# THE AURA

## Before Commencing Treatment

As before, ensure that you "set the scene" by selecting a quiet and comfortable healing space. You will not need a blanket to cover your client as you will be working by placing crystals at various positions around the body. The number of treatments needed will depend on the client and their individual problem(s). As a general guide, 4 to 8 sessions is standard. Both you, as the therapist, and the client will discuss together how many treatments are needed. The client will report how they are feeling and you will observe changes in the client's appearance, behaviour and general demeanour. If you are new to energy work and healing it may take you a while to sense changes in the energy field.

## The Aura & Balancing the Chakras

*What You Will Need;* Your chosen crystals for use on the chakras and 8 clear quartz crystals.

Begin by asking the client to lie on their back with their arms and legs slightly apart.

Place your chosen crystals on the chakras by following the section on "Healing by Using the Chakra System".

Now, place your clear quartz crystals in the following order and at least 5 cm away from the body:

- Above the crown.

- In between the feet

- One on the outside of each knee.

- One on the outside of each elbow.

- One on the outside of each shoulder.

*Treatment Time:* To begin with 30 minutes, working up to 55 minutes maximum. The clear quartz crystals will help support the healing and will help balance the chakras. The crystals are placed in such a way so as to support and amplify the healing of each other. Some people suggest it is necessary to use a pendulum to check to see if the chakras are balanced after a treatment. This is not necessary as the crystals will do all the work that is required at that particular time. If the chakra is too open or too closed it may take time to correct the imbalance and one must be careful not to rush this. The client may be holding onto thoughts and feelings, as well as physical illness, for a reason and we are not helping the client if we try to force this away before they are ready; we must be patient. The crystals which have supported and worked within the aura will also carry out subtle changes. Your clients will often report an increased *sense of wellbeing as the holes in the auric field are repaired.*

*Ending the Treatment:* Before ending the treatment it is important to smooth down the energy field. You do this by standing to the left of the client and making  a series of smooth, sweeping movements with your hands down towards the client's feet. You then move to the right side of the client and repeat the process. If the client is asleep, gently wake them up by touching their elbow and informing them that the treatment has ended.  The client may be a bit fuzzy headed so remember to give them time to gather their thoughts. Having a glass of water readily available is a good idea.

## Treating Low Energy

If a client reports, or if you sense that, the client has blocked or suppressed energy the following treatment will help release these blockages and, over time, restore vitality.

*What you will need:* 7 clear quartz points and your chosen crystal for the heart chakra; two large towels.

Begin by folding up the towels into quarters and placing them parallel, one against each foot. Place one clear quartz crystal on each towel with the point facing the foot. The purpose of this is to open up the foot chakra.  The foot chakra is one of the minor chakras of the body however, as with all of the chakras, it does play an important role. An imbalance in the foot chakra will result in a person displaying feelings of negativity, selfishness, childlike behaviour and an unwillingness to accept or carry out positive changes in one's life. When opening the foot chakra using crystals, the vibrational energy will channel right through the body, balancing and adjusting all of the chakras in turn.

Place your chosen crystal over the heart chakra.

Place 5 crystals around the head, in the following order, around 4 cm from the physical body:

- One above the crown.

- One parallel to each ear.

- One on each side between the ear and the crown.

*Treatment Time:* Please see above. The treatment time varies between 30 minutes and 55 minutes. When ending the treatment, carry out the aura smoothing exercise as described previously and end the treatment in the appropriate manner.

The crystals are placed in the positions mentioned above so as to gain maximum benefit from the energy of the crystals and to facilitate healing. I have already mentioned the benefits of opening up the foot chakra. The crystals positioned around the head help to relax the mind and repair damage to the emotional body of the aura. Many people with low energy, fibromyalgia and ME have very active minds and feel physically drained and tired all or most of the time. The heart is the emotional centre of the body and that is why a crystal is placed there.

# VOGEL WANDS

**V**ogel Wands were created by Marcel Vogel, a research scientist who was interested in developing a style of cutting quartz crystals so as to magnify their power for healing purposes. When using a Vogel Wand the intent of the user is very important. The thoughts, feelings and intent are transmitted down through the crystal to the receiver and amplified therefore, it is important the user works with the best intentions. Vogel wands must not be used for any negative practices; if the user attempts to work with a Vogel Wand in such a way the wand may shatter.

*Note: Vogel Wands should NEVER be used when carrying out healing work on children. This is because a child's etheric body has not been fully formed. The wand will be too powerful and may simply shatter or fall off the child if the user places the wand on them. Do not use these wands on any children under the age of 16. If a wand is used on a younger child there may be damage to the aura and healing work with other clear quartz crystals may be required. If you have worked on a child using a Vogel Wand, and are concerned that you have damaged the aura, you can check if to see if repair work is needed by feeling around the aura and noting any areas of heaviness or thickness and asking the client to report how they are feeling. One healing session should be sufficient to ensure that the aura has been repaired. This work should be carried out straight away if the client is feeling well enough or as soon as possible (within 24 hours) if the client is feeling dizzy, sick and generally out of sorts. It is important to carry out the repair healing work as soon as possible so as to prevent further damage within the aura.*

# USING VOGEL WANDS

**tend to use these wands for two main reasons:**

1. To help reduce pain: For clients who have muscular pain in a specific area or clients who experience headaches or migraines.

2. To amplify the work of other crystals: The method for doing this is described below.

Place the wand in the hand which is your main healing hand. This is the hand which you feel is the most sensitive or receptive to subtle changes in energy; reiki workers or other healers will know which hand works best for them. Place the wand between 5 and 10 cm from the body. Keep this position for several minutes. You may feel inclined to move the wand clockwise or anti-clockwise in small circular motions. If you move the wand clockwise, you are adding energy to the body and anti-clockwise you are removing negative energy from the body. To reduce pain you need to remove the negative energy from the body that is causing the pain, so work in an anti-clockwise direction.

To amplify the work of any other crystals simply point the Vogel Wand over the crystal and feel the vibrations increase. This is then transferred to the client. If the energy appears to be too powerful you can remove it by carrying out small circular motions in an anti-clockwise direction. If you are working with several crystals you can point the wand at the crystal in the centre, which in turn will amplify the energy and vibrations of the others.

Treatment Times: When working on a specific area – 10 to 15 minutes is sufficient. You can carry out a full body treatment by working over the main chakras which may take between 70 and 90 minutes maximum as this healing is quite powerful. End your treatment by brushing down the aura.

# THE HARA

This is the energy centre in the body and I believe that this book would not be complete without mentioning it. The hara contains a person's life purpose. If an individual loses their life purpose the physical body will wilt and eventually die. The main centre of the hara is just below the navel, around two and a half inches below the belly button. The hara is an energy ball which is golden in colour.

One point of the hara consists of a fine line which runs from the centre of the naval into the ground. This helps to keep the person connected to nature and this reinforces the need to be walking in the woods, or on a beach, and why we may take time to listen to the birds sing. The other point of the hara radiates from the centre of the naval straight upwards above the head and connects us to the divine. Just above the heart there is a major point which consists of a ball of white light which contains our emotions and all of the things and people we love. This emotional centre helps support our need to carry out our life purpose.

When carrying out our regular meditations, one may feel increased sensations such as a buzzing or tingling in the hara as the energy develops. The advantage of building energy in this centre is an increased level of physical energy, as well as a greater idea of your life purpose. You will feel more in line with the universal life force and life will generally seem easier for you as you follow your natural path.

# DEVELOPING YOURSELF

**N**ow that you have a greater level of awareness of the subtle energy systems of the body and how crystals can facilitate healing and increase ones vibrational energy, you may wish to develop yourself further.

Intuitively, given time, you will know your right path. Some walk down the path of psychic development others choose the path leading to energy work, including reiki. This is where I began my journey and with time, self- healing and lots of meditation, I have finally opened my own school of reiki. If you are interested in learning more about reiki or would like to take a course with me at The British Academy Of Reiki please have a look at my website: www.britishacademyofreiki.co.uk . If you have any questions or comments I would be delighted to hear from you. Please feel free to email me at: marionreiki@yahoo.co.uk